I V O R Y
EXALTATION

Arrangements
for the
Advanced Pianist

BY MARILYNN HAM

Lillenas Publishing Co.
KANSAS CITY, MO. 64141

Contents

With all my love to my husband, Bob

Advent Medley

(*with* We Shall Behold Him)

(Narration to be read prior to the performance of this arrangement)

This arrangement ties together Christ's first and second advents by contrasting the roles of the stars, as depicted in two well-loved songs. The carol, "Away in a Manger," states that when Jesus came to earth to be born as a baby, "The stars in the sky looked down where He lay, the little Lord Jesus asleep on the hay." But contrast this quiet scene with the awesome glory of His triumphant return to earth a second time. In the song, "We Shall Behold Him," Dottie Rambo writes, "The stars shall applaud Him with thunders of praise . . . and we shall behold Him then face to face." With the playing of this arrangement we want to follow the instructions of the Apostle Paul when he wrote, ". . . let us encourage one another—and all the more as you see the Day approaching" (Heb. 10:25b, NIV).

Arr. by Marilynn Ham

Steady, but growing in intensity and volume

*Accelerate into the trill—unmeasured.

With all my love to my son, Norris.

Children's Medley

Arr. by Marilynn Ham

Moderato—Gently

"Sonata in C Major, K. 545" (Mozart)

"Praise Him, All Ye Little Children" (Anonymous)

*"Music Box Dancer" (Frank Mills)

12

"Jesus Loves Me" (Bradbury)

In loving memory of my dear uncle, Dr. Robert White,
whose love for the great anthems of the church inspired this arrangement.

Exalt Him with Song

Arr. by Marilynn Ham

Marcato ♩ = 69
"All Creatures of Our God and King" (from *Geistliche Kirchengesäng*, 1623)

17

*With special thanks to Rowena Holliday for her help and encouragement
in preparing these manuscripts.*

His Eye Is on the Sparrow

CHARLES H. GABRIEL
Arr. by Marilynn Ham

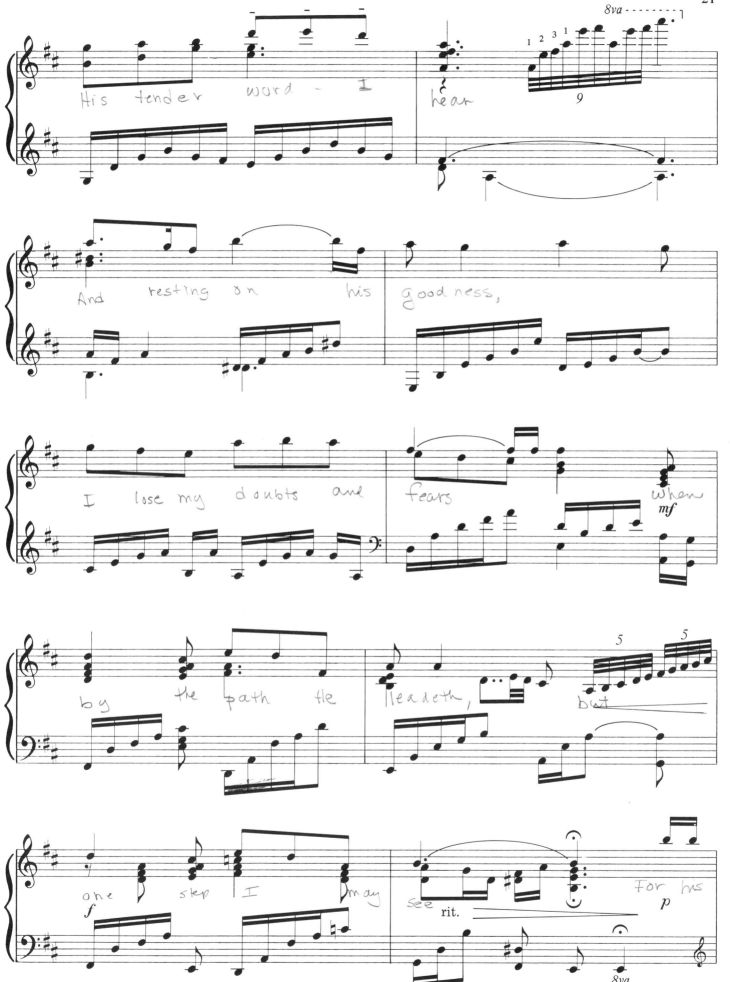

His ten-der word—I hear

And rest-ing on his good-ness,

I lose my doubts and fears

When

by the path He lead-eth,

but

one step I may

see

For his

22

To Susan Riley, with thanks for all the work put into these manuscripts.

Great Is Thy Faithfulness

WILLIAM M. RUNYAN
Arr. by Marilynn Ham

Dedicated to Janice Bridges, who always appreciated the message of the hymn, "Be Still, My Soul."

Be Still, My Soul

(*with* **Where the Spirit of the Lord Is**)

Arr. by Marilynn Ham

*"Where the Spirit of the Lord Is" (Adams)

To my dear pastors and friends, Gary and Carol Wright.

Love Medley

Arr. by Marilynn Ham

Like beginning

en-ter every | trembling | heart

*"O How He Loves You and Me" (Kaiser)

Slower

"My Jesus, I
Love Thee"
(Gordon)

To Mom, for her musical and godly influence on my life.

And Can It Be?

THOMAS CAMPBELL
Arr. by Marilynn Ham

For Sheryl Smith Mullikin, my student, friend, and the first to perform one of my arrangements.

Praise Medley

Arr. by Marilynn Ham

Rhythmically ♩ = 100
*"I Just Came to Praise the Lord" (Romero)

Ragtime style, softly

cresc. poco a poco

"To God Be the Glory"
(Doane)

8va

With deepest gratitude to Dr. George Whitfield, my piano teacher, for his faith in me.

Amazing Grace

(With ASH GROVE)

Early American Melody
Arr. by Marilynn Ham